Mandala

Coloring Book

For Adult

Relaxation

Your rating

Your rating

☆☆☆☆☆

Your rating

Your rating

Your rating

☆☆☆☆☆

Your rating

☆☆☆☆☆

Your rating

☆☆☆☆☆

Your rating

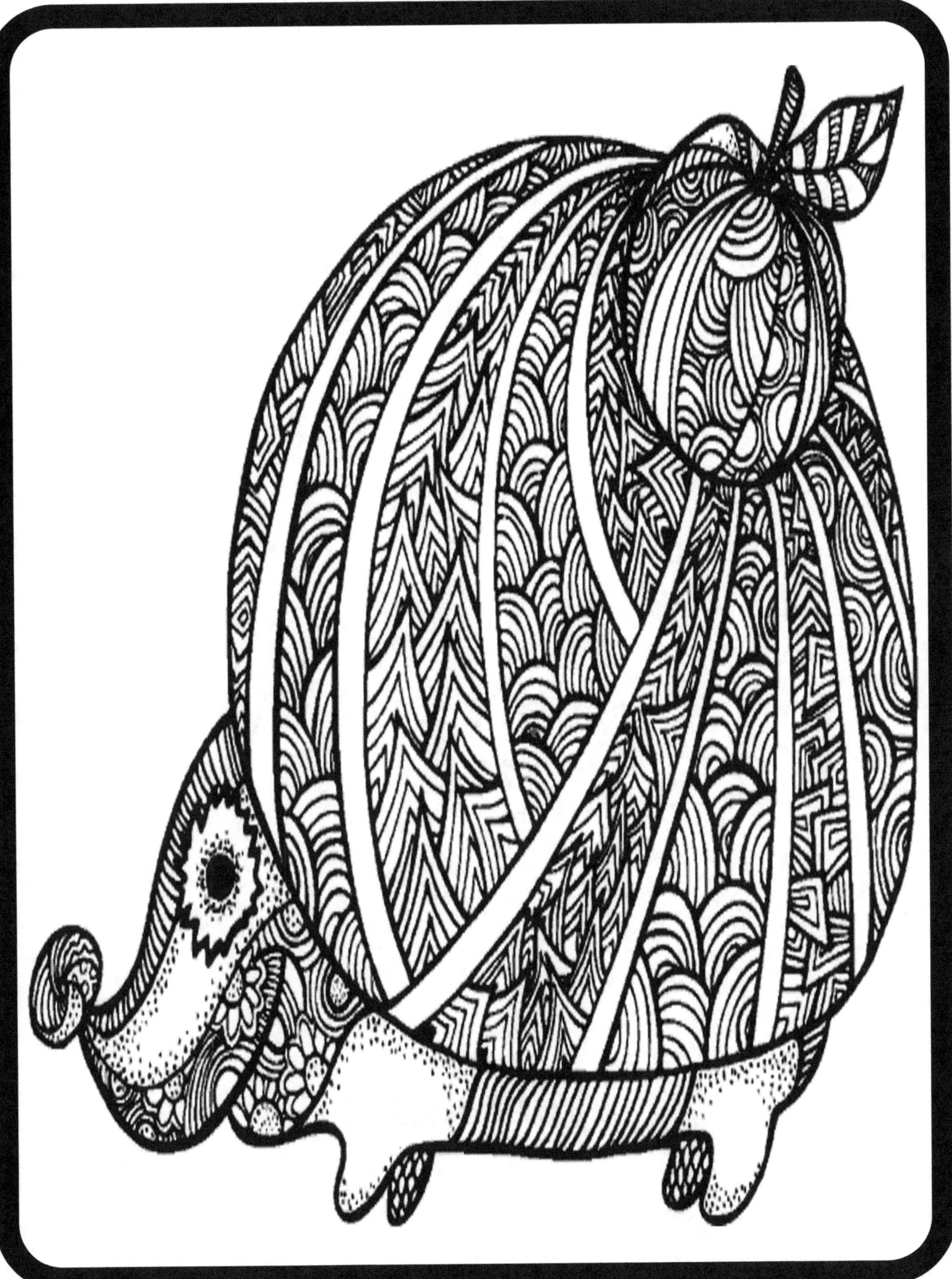

Your rating

Your rating

☆ ☆ ☆ ☆ ☆

Your rating

Your rating

Your rating

Your rating

Your rating

☆☆☆☆☆

Your rating

Your rating

Your rating

Your rating

Your rating

Your rating

Your rating

Your rating

Your rating

Your rating

Your rating

Your rating

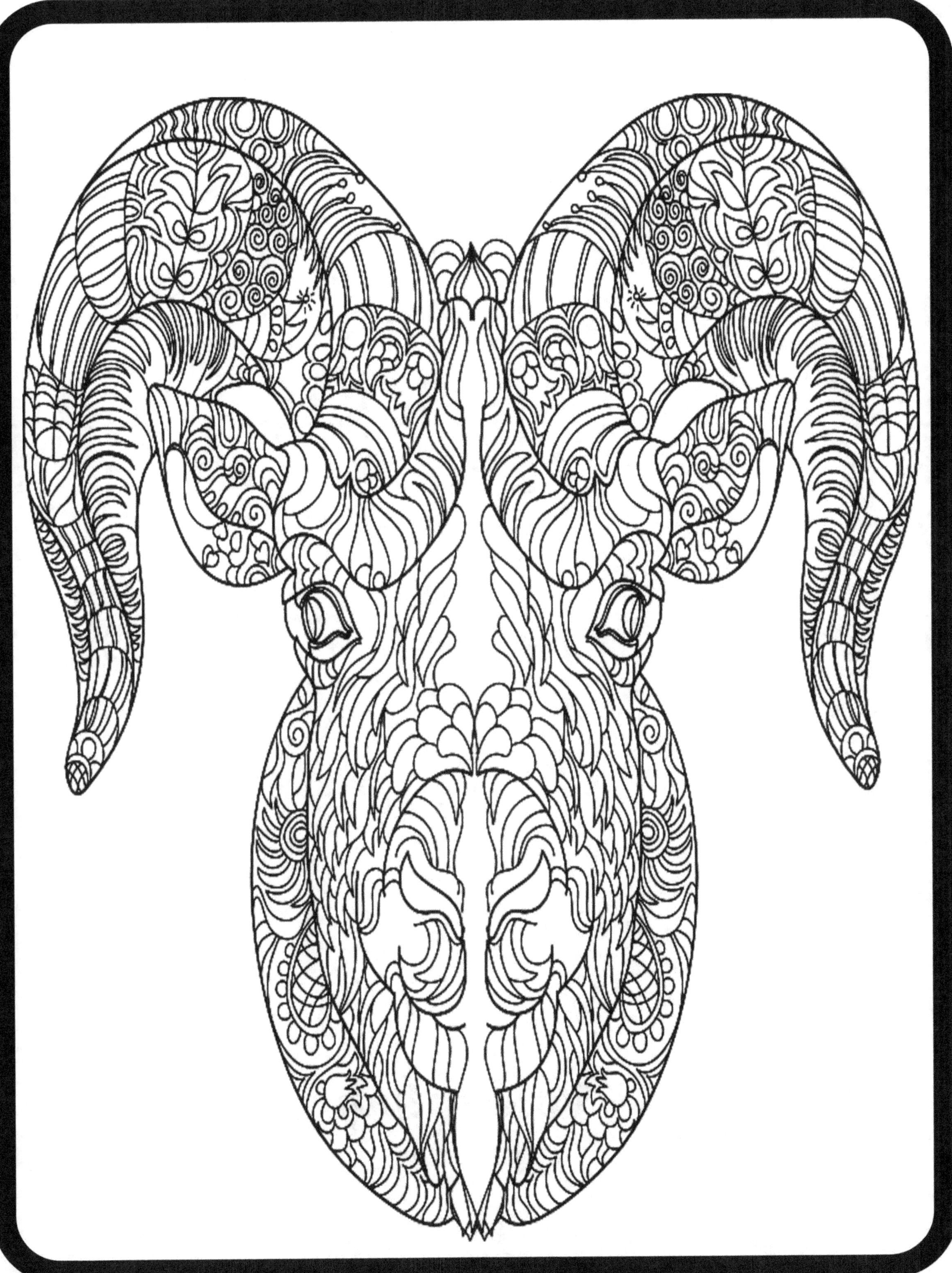

Your rating

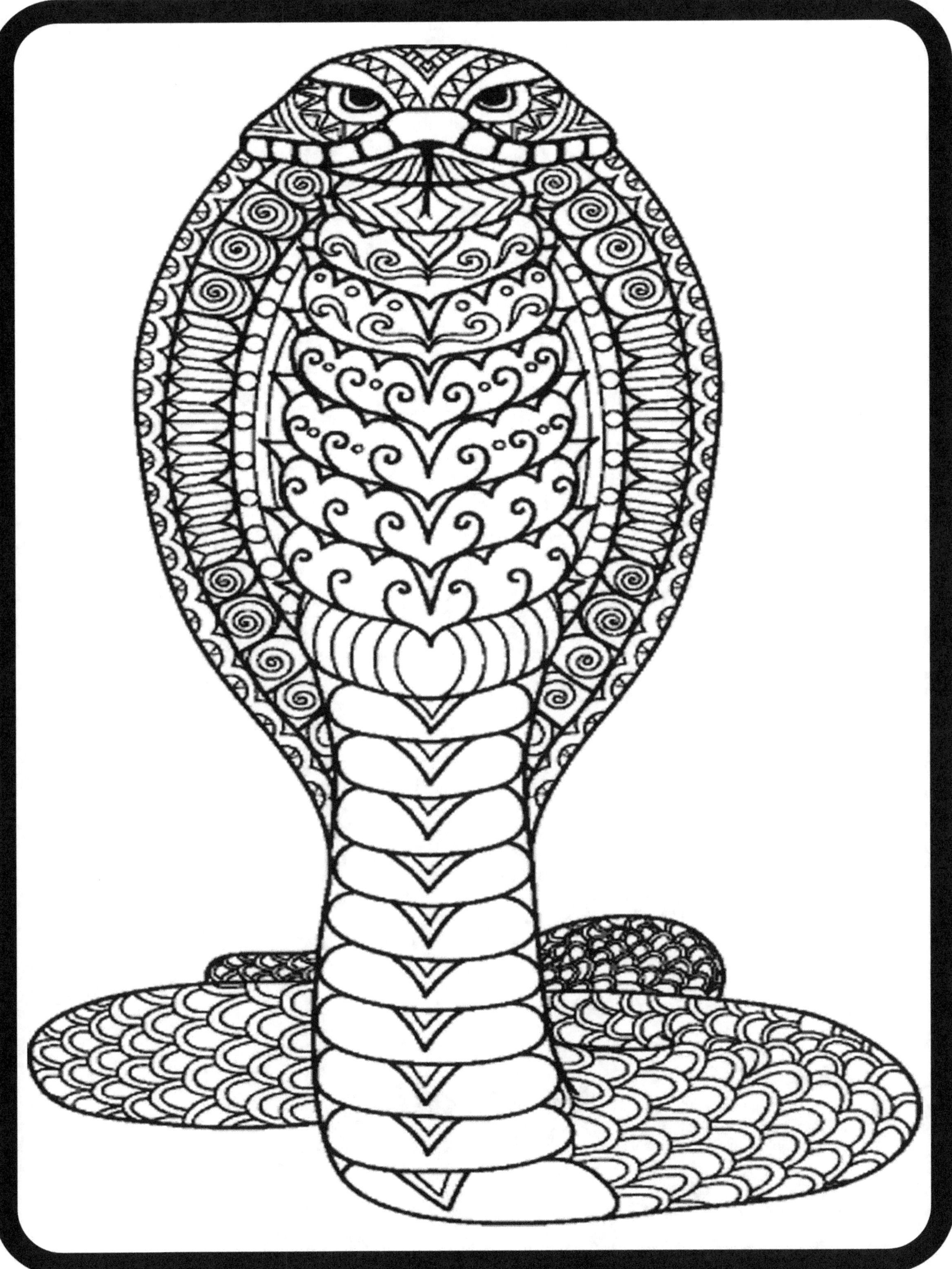

Your rating

Your rating

☆☆☆☆☆

Your rating

Your rating

Your rating

Your rating

Your rating

Your rating

Your rating

Your rating

Your rating

Your rating

Your rating

☆☆☆☆☆

Your rating

Your rating

☆☆☆☆☆

Your rating

Your rating

☆☆☆☆☆

Your rating

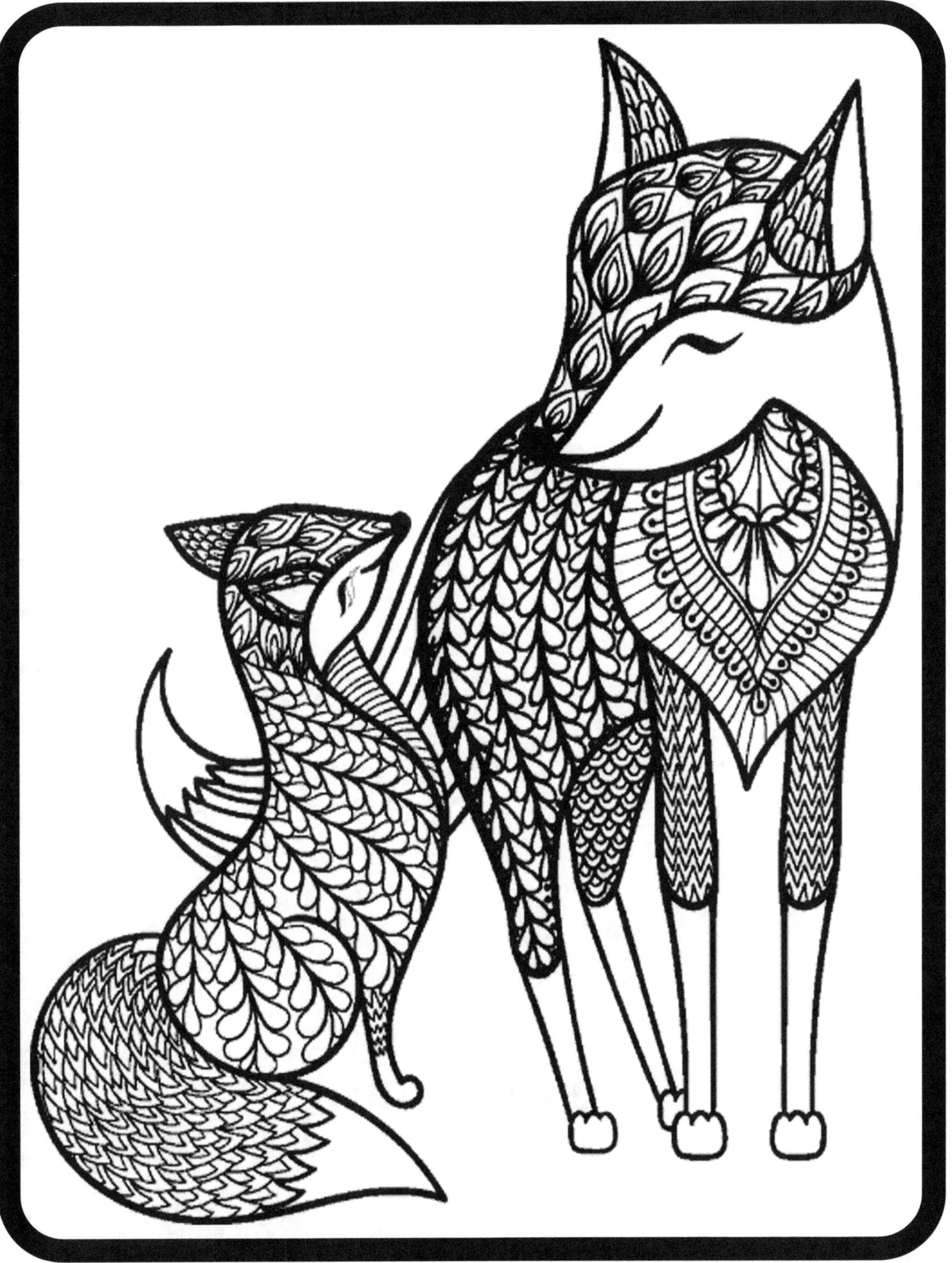

Your rating

Your rating

Your rating

☆ ☆ ☆ ☆ ☆

Your rating

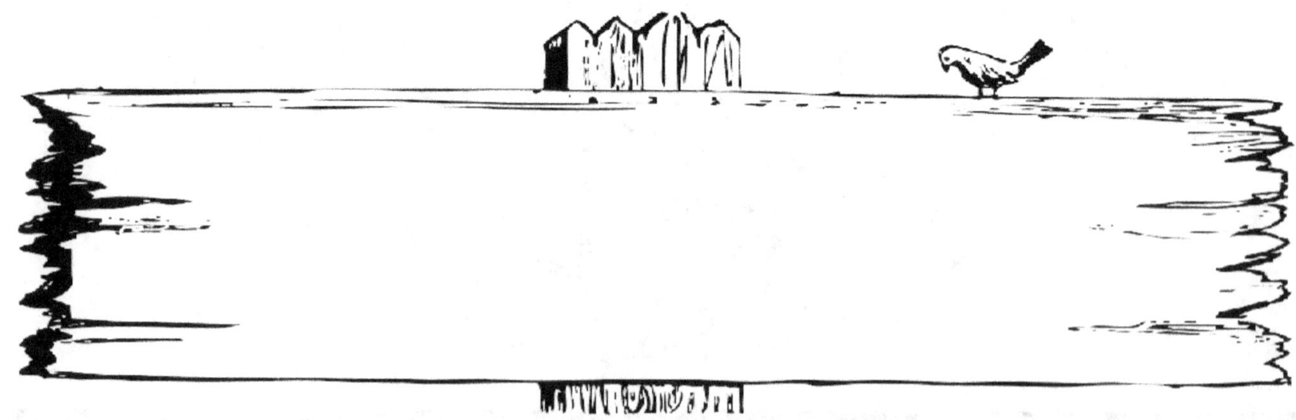

THANK YOU